C000244075

The Little Recognized Secret of Success

Dale Carnegie

THE LITTLE RECOGNIZED SECRET OF SUCCESS

By Dale Carnegie

One morning years ago, I walked across the campus of the State Teachers' College at Warrensburg, Missouri, and stopped to chat with a friend of mine—Frank Self. Little did I realize then, that that chat was to have a profound effect upon all the days of my years.

If I had not met Frank Self that morning, I would probably have been a superintendent of some high school or college in the Middle West, for I had spent four years in a college for training teachers.

During our talk, Frank Self told me that the previous summer he had been selling courses for the International Correspondence Schools. I was astounded when he told me that they paid him two dollars a day for hotel expenses and a commission for all courses he sold. Two dollars a day for hotel expenses! The very thought of it excited me.

Two dollars a day was all I could hope to make as a teacher in some country town and out of that two dollars I would have to pay room and board. Here was a way to make money quickly! I wondered how long this kind of high finance had been going on.

It couldn't be done—but I didn't know that!

The nearest office of the International Correspondence Schools was in Denver. I had never been in a big city. I didn't know that I couldn't get a position with I.C.S. by merely writing a letter to the Denver office of the company. Since I was too dumb to know it couldn't be done—I did it. I learned afterwards that I got the position solely because I had told in my letter that I had won first honors in several public speaking and debating contests in college. The International Correspondence Schools felt that a lad who could win debates in school ought to be able to sell anything!

I go from farming to selling

So, I left the farm forever. That morning I entered a new world—a world where there were no cows to milk, no weeds to destroy, no wood to cut, no cow manure to be pitched out of the cow shed—a strange world—a competitive and tough world—the world of selling.

The first night in Denver, I slept in a shabby, furnished room above a grocery store. I paid a quarter or maybe fifty cents for it. I had been warned about "city slickers." I *knew* that the big cities were full of gangsters and pickpockets just waiting for a farm boy like me. I had twenty-eight dollars pinned in a little cloth bag which my mother made. It hung around my neck under my shirt.

A bad night in a big city

I was afraid to turn out the light for fear I might be robbed. A few hours later, I awoke with a start. Someone was pounding on my door. The city slickers were after me! "Here I am," I said to myself, "being robbed —maybe murdered the first night in a big city." When

I discovered that it was merely the night watchman ordering me to turn out the light, I could have buried my head under the bedclothes in embarrassment.

I started as a salesman a few days later. I was given a territory among the sand hills of Western Nebraska—an impossible territory. My headquarters were at Alliance. Charles Schwab himself couldn't have sold educational courses to the potato farmers and ranchers among the sand hills of Western Nebraska. I was desperate. Here I was, failing at the first job I had after college. I was so desperate that I even stopped cattle ranchers on the streets to ask them if they didn't want to study electrical engineering by correspondence. As I look back at it now, it seems like something out of Gilbert and Sullivan.

I sell my first, last and only I.C.S. Course!

Someone told me of a ranch hand seven miles out in the country who was interested in getting more education. Since I couldn't afford to hire a team of livery stable horses to take me out to my prospect, I walked the seven miles. What happened? Nothing! All I got out of it was sore feet. I went back to my lonely room and threw myself across the bed and wept in despair. I was ashamed to go home and admit that I had failed in my first undertaking. I hated to keep on and I hated to stop. I saw a man painting a barn. I tried to sell him a course in sign painting. He thought I was being funny. I saw a lineman climbing a telephone pole. I pleaded with him to become an electrical engineer by mail. Since he was up a pole and couldn't get away from me, he began asking questions. He took me to his home. His mother and father urged him to get more education. So he bought a course—electrical engineering —and paid me $88 cash for it—the first and only one I ever sold for the International Correspondence Schools.

I shall always be grateful to a cracker salesman I met one night in a grocery store in Scottsbluff, Nebraska. When I told him what I was doing, he said: "Son, you haven't got a real job at all. You don't have any repeat sales." He told me to get a job selling some food product for which there was a demand. I resolved then and there that I would get a job selling ham and bacon and lard for Armour or Swift.

I ride to Omaha with a carload of horses

Since I hadn't the money to buy a ticket to Omaha, I had to figure out a way to get there without cash. I knew that if a farmer shipped a carload of cattle or hogs or horses, he got two tickets free, so I went to the stockyards in Alliance, Nebraska, and found a man who was shipping a carload of range horses to Omaha and told him that, if he would give me a ticket, I would help him water and feed the horses and keep them on their feet so they wouldn't be trampled to death.

I wanted a job selling bacon and lard and soap for Armour or Swift. I realized that I didn't know how to apply for a job, so to get some experience in applying for a job, I stopped on my way to South Omaha and applied for a job that I really didn't want at all—a job as traveling salesman for a wholesale hardware company. I didn't get the job, but I did get the experience I needed.

Armour & Company takes a chance

When I arrived in South Omaha, both Cudahy and the Omaha Packing Company felt that they could struggle along somehow without my services as a salesman. But the sales manager of Armour & Company, Rufus E. Harris, was a reckless man. He took chances. He hired me to sell bacon and ham and beef, canned meats and cheese to butcher shops and grocery stores in South Dakota. Armour had 27 traveling men selling Armour products in the Midwest. My salary was seventeen dollars and thirty-one cents a week! Plus traveling expenses! When I wrote the thrilling news to my parents, they could hardly believe it. There had been periods on the farm when father hadn't made that much in an entire year. Father warned me that Armour & Company couldn't keep on paying that much money very long. I feared he was right.

My territory covered practically all of the state of South Dakota—from the Minnesota line to the Black Hills. For some unknown reason, every salesman who had tried to sell Armour products in that territory had failed. It now stood at the very bottom of the 27 sales territories handled by the South Omaha branch. That was the reason I got it.

5

Within two years, I raised that territory from 27th place to first place. The day I received a letter of congratulations from my boss saying, "You have achieved what seemed impossible," I had to go out and buy a bigger hat.

Six months later, when I was twenty-two, Armour offered to make me manager of their branch house in Des Moines, Iowa. They told me I was the youngest man who had ever been offered such a position by Armour & Company. I didn't accept because I had already decided to come to New York to study at the American Academy of Dramatic Arts.

(I was on the stage for one year. Let us pass over that year in the silence it deserves.)

Enthusiasm does the trick

Whatever success I had as an Armour salesman was due almost entirely to my enthusiasm, my eagerness to work day and night to make good. I was determined to make good no matter what the cost, because I knew that, if I failed, I would have had to go home and admit failure in the first real job I ever had. Besides, my work was far more interesting and far more lucrative than milking cows, shucking corn and cleaning out the henhouse on the farm.

I was so excited I probably worked harder than other salesmen in South Dakota. I had to travel on the caboose of freight trains. While the train was switching cars and unloading freight, I would run uptown and call on the butcher shops and grocery stores. I'll bet the townspeople got many a smile out of my coattail flying in the winds as I dashed back to the moving train and swung on to the platform. The wonder was that I didn't lose my grip and slip under the train and lose a leg.

From a hundred above to forty below!

In summer, the heat rose to over a hundred on the sun-parched plains; and in the winter the thermometer registered forty below zero.

One day the snow was so deep and the cold so intense that even a freight wouldn't run.

However, I didn't know it, so I dashed down to the depot as usual and in that ten-minute run, I froze both my ears. Scores of microscopic blood vessels in my ears burst. The wonder is that I didn't lose both ears. They were injured so severely that almost a half a century later my ears pained me on a cold day so I had to walk down the street with my hands cupped over them.

Why am I telling you all this? Simply because I hope it shows that my determination to make good was so intense that nothing could stop me.

Enthusiasm worked miracles for me

I regret to say that I did not inherit any superior intelligence from my ancestors, but I did develop a superior enthusiasm from my mother. Is enthusiasm important in selling? Yes, real, honest, genuine, heartfelt enthusiasm is one of the most potent factors of success in almost any undertaking.

Charles Schwab—a man who was paid a salary of a million dollars a year—told me that the secret of his success was enthusiasm. He declared that a man can succeed at almost anything for which he has unlimited enthusiasm.

I once interviewed Frederick Williamson on a radio program. He was, at that time, president of the New York Central Railway. When I asked for his recipe for success, he said: "The longer I live, the more certain I am that enthusiasm is the little-recognized secret of success. The difference in actual skill and ability and intelligence between those who succeed and those who fail is usually neither wide nor striking. But if two men are nearly equally matched, the man who is enthusiastic will find the scales tipped in his favor. And a man of second-rate ability with enthusiasm will often outstrip one of first-rate ability without enthusiasm."

"Emotional drive" is what counts!

Once I heard a famous psychologist, in discussing Army aptitude tests, remark that I.Q. tests have one important shortcoming. They fail to measure "emotional drive." According to I.Q. tests, a man with a low score is usually rated as fit for only menial jobs, while a high score is considered practically a guarantee of success. You and I know how misleading that is. I have seen men with low I.Q.'s suddenly "set on fire" by a new idea or a new line of work. It gives them "emotional drive," which sends them on to great success. And I have seen men with high I.Q.'s fail miserably.

When Mark Twain was asked the reason for his success, he replied: "I was born excited."

The late William Lyon Phelps, one of the most popular teachers in the history of Yale, told me almost the same thing. Professor Phelps even wrote a book entitled *The Excitement of Teaching*. On Page 21 of that book, he said: "With me, teaching is more than an art or an occupation. It is a passion. I love to teach as a painter loves to paint, as a singer loves to sing, as a poet loves to write. Before I get out of bed in the morning, I think with ardent delight of my first group of students.

"One of the chief reasons for success in life is the ability to maintain a daily interest in one's work, to have a chronic enthusiasm; to regard each day as important."

That is one of the chief reasons for success in any undertaking—yes, that is true, even of salesmen!

One summer evening, several years ago, I studied the salesmanship of two star-gazing merchants who had set up telescopes at 42nd Street, opposite the Public Library in New York. One charged ten cents for a look at the moon. The other man, who had a slightly larger telescope, charged a quarter.

The man who charged a quarter a look was getting four times as many customers as the man who charged only ten cents. To be sure, you got a slightly better view with the twenty-five-cent telescope—but the main reason for the financial success of this higher priced telescope was the personality of the man in charge of it. He radiated enthusiasm. He talked about looking

9

at the moon with such excitement, that one would, if necessary, have passed up his dinner in order to see it. The man with the ten-cent telescope said nothing. He merely took orders.

This experience was to me an astronomical example of the value of enthusiasm.

When Sir Edward Victor Appleton, who had been knighted by the King of England and awarded the Nobel Prize in Physics—when this great scientist was made Chancellor of the University of Edinburgh, Time magazine sent him a wireless message asking him if he had any recipe for success. "Yes," he replied, "enthusiasm. I rate that even ahead of professional skill."

Enthusiasm rates first

I don't know of anything in the world that will do more for you than enthusiasm. Thomas A. Edison said: "When a man dies, if he can pass enthusiasm along to his children, he has left them an estate of incalculable value." Experience proves that to be true. It is more than wealth, for enthusiasm will produce wealth. Not only wealth but a great zest for living.

Ralph Waldo Emerson, who is considered the greatest of American philosophers, saw the value of enthusiasm. In one of his essays he wrote: "Every great and commanding moment in the annals of the world is the triumph of some enthusiasm."

Two men in an office have exactly the same kind of jobs. One works at his in a half-hearted way, as if bored by it and glad to have the hands of the clock point to five. The other does his work with gusto. He finds it exciting, finds each day an adventure. Now which do you think is going to do better work? Which one is going to get ahead?

John James Audubon was the greatest naturalist that America has ever produced, and the great thing that he passed on to this country was his bird drawings. Some of them have sold for as high as $5,000. He would disappear into the wilderness and be gone for months. But he would return with more wonderful drawings of birds. Once when he came back, he opened his trunk where he had stored his precious drawings, and found that the rats had been among them and had gnawed and defaced them, destroying the work of months. A friend offered solace for the blow. But solace wasn't necessary for Audubon. He said: "They have destroyed my drawings. They haven't destroyed my enthusiasm."

And they had not, for he went ahead and produced, after that, some of his greatest watercolors.

Charles F. Kettering, the great inventor, said: "We are just coming into an era where in every conceivable field, there are opportunities such as were never dreamed of. These opportunities will go to the men and women who have enthusiasm."

During World War I, Alexander de Seversky went up in a fighting plane on his first trip. He had been up only a few minutes when he was shot down and fell into the Gulf of Riga. Picked up by a Russian battleship, he was rushed to a hospital where a leg was amputated. When he again became conscious, they asked him what he wanted to do. He said: "I want to fly."

That is enthusiasm, the enthusiasm that accomplishes.

But enthusiasm is more than just zest for work. It is for the whole of life and living. If you have it, you have a priceless possession. Cherish it.

Recommended Readings

- Riches Are Your Right by Joseph Murphy

- The Money Illusion by Irving Fisher

- How To Win Friends And Influence People: A Condensation From The Book by Dale Carnegie

- Praying the Psalms by Thomas Merton

- The Magic of Believing by Claude M. Bristol

- Scientific Advertising by Claude C. Hopkins

- The Law of Success: Using the Power of Spirit to Create Health, Prosperity, and Happiness by Paramahansa Yogananda

- Five Minute Biographies by Dale Carnegie by Dale Carnegie

- The Dale Carnegie Course on Effective Speaking, Personality Development, and the Art of How to Win Friends & Influence People

- Little Known Facts About Well Known People by Dale Carnegie

- Dale Carnegie's Radio Program: How to Win Friends and Influence People Lesson 1: Gain insight into handling difficult people; Discover the keys to popularity; What employers want in their employees
by Dale Carnegie and Jason McCoy (Narrator)

Available at bnpublishing.com

Get Published!

"Everyone has something they know well or can do well. And when a person has a skill, there's always going to be someone willing to pay for it."

— *bnpublishing.com*

BN Publishing helps authors publish more titles. So whether you're writing a romance novel, a historical fiction, a mystery, action or suspense story, poetry, about business, a children's book, or any other, we can help you reach your publishing goals.

Besides telling a story, a book is a promotional tool. A book can be likened to a powerful business card since most people won't throw it out. Authoring a book can give you credibility and status, enabling you to charge more for your services.
With our best resources, we will help expose your talent to the public and publish your book for FREE!

Your writing will reach 20,000 retail accounts in the United States (chains, independents, specialty stores, and libraries), including:

www.amazon.com

www.amazon.co.uk

www.amazon.ca

www.bn.com

www.powells.com

www.ebay.com

and more...

Your book will be also included in a physical catalog which goes out to retail stores. Furthermore, when your title is entered into our library, it will automatically appear in bookstore and library databases.

Our United States- and United Kingdom-based sales teams work with clients all over the world through our broad distribution channel partners.

For more information please contact

editor@bnpublishing.net

Printed in the USA
CPSIA information can be obtained
at www.ICGtesting.com
LVHW091429110424
777117LV00002B/392